Long Covid - The Long Covid Book for Clinicians and Sufferers - Away from Despair and Towards Understanding

Jean-Maurice Cecilia-Menzel

Published by Jean-Maurice Cecilia-Menzel, 2022.

While every precaution has been taken in the preparation of this book, the publisher assumes no responsibility for errors or omissions, or for damages resulting from the use of the information contained herein.

LONG COVID - THE LONG COVID BOOK FOR CLINICIANS AND SUFFERERS - AWAY FROM DESPAIR AND TOWARDS UNDERSTANDING

First edition. October 24, 2022.

ISBN: 979-8215815625

Written by Jean-Maurice Cecilia-Menzel.

Imprint

Jean-Maurice Cecilia-Menzel

Medical practitioner for psychotherapy

Hildeboldstrasse 1, 80797, Munich

telephone: 089 44135911

e-mail: info@neurofeedback-praxis-muenchen.de

Competent supervisory authority:

Public Health Office Munich

Professional liability insurance with

Hiscox SA, Branch Office for Germany

Chief representative: Robert Dietrich

Arnulfstrasse 31

80636 Munich

Tel.: +49 89 54 58 01 281

Responsible tax office

Tax office Munich

Table of Contents

Chapter 1 Background of Long COVID
Overview of Long COVID

COVID-19 or SARS-CoV-2 infection emerged as a global pandemic, associated with increased morbidity and mortality across the globe. The symptoms of COVID-19 appear 4-5 days following the exposure. The symptoms include throat pain, body aches, fever, cough, diarrhea, and loss of smell and taste. In the case of -mild infection, one may recover 7-10 days following the occurrence of symptoms while in severe cases, the recovery period may last for 3-6 weeks. Despite recovering from the COVID-19 infection, some individuals report the persistence of symptoms, usually weeks and even months after the infection. Such individuals are commonly labeled as long haulers.

Long haulers are considered to be suffering from long COVID or post-COVID syndrome. This health condition is characterized by the presence of symptoms weeks or months following the initial onset of the infection. In addition to the persistence of older symptoms, some new symptoms may also develop in the case of long COVID. The development of this condition is not associated with the viral status in the body. This means that an individual may have long COVID even if the body has eradicated the virus, as indicated by the polymerase chain reaction (PCR) test. In other words, long COVID is the period from microbiological recovery to clinical recovery. (Raveendran et al., 2021)

Based on the duration of the presence of symptoms, long COVID can be categorized into post-acute COVID stage and chronic COVID stage. In the post-acute COVID stage of long COVID, the duration of symptoms ranges from 3 weeks to 12 weeks. The chronic COVID stage occurs when the symptoms are present longer than a period of 12 weeks. The symptoms may be relapsing (worsening) or remitting (repeating) in the case of long COVID. This chapter provides insight into the symptoms, risk factors, pathogenesis, diagnosis, and an overview of treatment options for long COVID. Basic knowledge of these topics is essential for understanding and adapting to the strategies for self-management of long COVID.

Post-Viral Fatigue Syndrome

Post-viral fatigue syndrome, clinically known as myalgic encephalomyelitis, is characterized by a lack of energy, exhaustion, weakness, or tiredness following a viral infection. Formerly known as Royal Free disease and Iceland disease, post-viral fatigue syndrome is a significant occurrence in epidemics. Research studies suggest that post-viral fatigue syndrome is a metabolic disorder, which occurs following a persistent viral infection. With reference to SARS-CoV-2 infection, the post-COVID-19 fatigue syndrome (PCFS) arises in the presence of different triggering factors. Emotional trauma, vaccinations, and emotional trauma share similar traits with a physiological stressor – SARS-CoV-2 infection.

PCFS is associated with neuroinflammation, characterized by the activation of an innate immune response in the brain. This manifests as the key symptoms of PCFS including depression, pain, fatigue, and cognitive impairment. Exposure to environmental, emotional, and physical stressors in individuals who are already subjected to a severe physiologic stressor leads to hypothalamic dysfunction, which triggers neuroinflammation and subsequent PCFS symptoms. PCFS is a clinically significant health problem, increasing the health burden in the background of the COVID-19 pandemic. Drugs mediating inflammation are potentially beneficial for alleviating the symptoms of PCFS.

The Symptoms of Long COVID

Individuals suffering from long COVID report the presence of 1 or more symptoms. The common symptoms among long haulers include breathlessness, chest pain, profound fatigue, palpitations, cough, myalgia, muscle weakness, chest pain, joint pain, insomnia, headache, paresthesia (pins and needles), hair loss, rash, diarrhea, problems with concentration and memory, improper gait, impaired balance, and poor quality of life. Some symptoms initially appear 3-4 weeks following the occurrence2 of acute symptoms. About a quarter of individuals suffering from long COVID exhibit painful symptoms. The two patterns of the symptoms of long COVID are as follows.

1. Headache, upper respiratory problems (sore throat, loss of the sensation of smell, shortness of breath, and persistent cough), and fatigue.
2. Fever, gastroenterological symptoms, and other multi-system complaints.

Profound fatigue is prevalent among individuals who recover from the initial infection but continue to experience remitting and relapsing symptoms. Females and individuals with a diagnosis of anxiety or depression are more likely to experience profound fatigue. Multi-system complaints associated with SARS-CoV-2 infection include pulmonary, cardiac, and neurological complications. (Crook et al., 2021)

The pulmonary complications include chronic cough, post-COVID fibrosis, pulmonary vascular disease, and bronchiectasis. Residual pulmonary involvement may lead to the chronic onset of shortness of breath. However, the majority of asymptomatic individuals demonstrate significant involvement of the lungs. Pulmonary fibrosis associated with COVID-19 leads to the persistence of dyspnea, and the affected individuals may require supplementary oxygen.

Cardiac complications associated with COVID-19 include myocarditis, pericarditis, an abnormal response of blood pressure and heart rate to activity, impairment of myocardial flow reserve, myocardial infarction, arrhythmias, sudden cardiac death, and cardiac failure. Individuals who recovered from SARS-CoV-2 infection are also subject to changes in the functional and structural integrity of the brain. Common neurological symptoms of long COVID include cognitive blunting or brain fog, headache, peripheral nerve dysfunction, tremor, concentration and attention difficulties, and mental health conditions.

The above-mentioned symptoms and complications, in addition to inflammatory arthralgia, venous thrombosis, and arterial thrombosis, are manifestations observed in long haulers.

Who is at Risk for Long COVID?

The following are different factors that contribute to the increased risk of developing long COVID.

1. Women are at a greater risk for long COVID as compared to men
2. Increasing age is positively associated with the onset of long COVID
3. The onset of greater than 5 symptoms during acute COVID increases the risk for long COVID
4. Comorbidities also increase the likelihood of the development of long COVID

Causes of Long COVID

Over the course of the pandemic, different theories have been developed to evaluate the underlying cause of long COVID and why some individuals fully recover from COVID while symptoms persist in others. Researchers found traces of viral proteins and viral ribonucleic acid (RNA) in the body tissues, while some COVID patients harbored the viral RNA or proteins in the body tissues. This lingering virus may be a potential source of the development of long COVID, however, deeper and more thorough studies are required to assess the onset of long COVID and the persistence of symptoms, which are associated with the lingering viral components in the body.

Pathogenesis of Long COVID

Mechanisms underlying the presence, relapse, and remitting of symptoms in individuals who recovered from the SARS-CoV-2 infection are listed as follows.

1. Secondary to organ damage that occurred during the infection
2. The extent or magnitude of organ damage during the infection
3. Time duration for the recovery of organ damage
4. The continuous onset of chronic inflammation
5. Persistence of immune response or generation of autoantibodies
6. Persistence of virus in the tissues in rare cases
7. Outcome of hospitalization
8. Sequela of a severe health condition
9. Adverse effects of pharmacological intervention in SARS-CoV-2 infection
10. Post-intensive care syndrome
11. Complications associated with SARS-CoV-2 infection
12. Complications associated with comorbidities
13. Persistence of viremia in individuals with relapse, altered immunity, and re-infection
14. Psychological problems, including post-traumatic stress
15. Financial and social outcomes associated with COVID-19

As per the perspective of public health practices, it is important to distinguish between re-infection and the onset of residual symptoms of the disease. Persistent elevation of inflammatory markers in the body reflects the chronic presence of inflammation. Moreover, the reactivation of Epstein-Barr virus (EBV) and the pre-existing onset of diabetes mellitus during acute SARS-CoV-2 infection also contribute to the development of long COVID. SARS-CoV-2 viremia is proportional to the viral burden in the body tissues and subsequent end-organ damage. Residual inflammation and microvascular dysregulation are also important factors, which contribute to the development of long COVID. (Yan et al., 2021)

What is the Neurobiology of Long COVID?

Long COVID is associated with neurological manifestations related to the central nervous system (CNS) and peripheral nervous system (PNS). The non-specific neurological symptoms of long COVID such as sleep disorders, postexertional malaise, fatigue, and brain fog represent the existence of disorders associated with other organ systems. These disorders may include endocrine, respiratory, renal, cardiovascular, autoimmune, psychiatric, and hematologic pathologies. Neurological symptoms of long COVID associated with the CNS are sleep disorders, dizziness, emotional or mood disorders, fatigue, headache, brain fog, dysautonomia, and cognitive impairment. In contrast, neurological symptoms of long COVID associated with PNS are muscle weakness, tinnitus, hearing loss, myalgias, sensorimotor deficits including dysesthesia, tremor, hypoesthesia, hypogeusia, and hyposmia.

The pathophysiological mechanisms underlying neurological manifestations of long COVID include viral neuroinvasion, dysfunction of the blood-brain barrier associated with endotheliopathy, aberrant responses of the immune system, coagulopathies in association with ischemic neuronal injury, cellular apoptosis, metabolic imbalances, and oxidative stress.

Diagnosis of Long COVID

The diagnosis of long COVID involves detailed history followed by a thorough clinical examination in individuals with prior SARS-CoV-2 infection. The lack of evidence related to prior SARS-CoV-2 infection along with the demonstration of symptoms associated with long COVID may require a positive antibody test to confirm the diagnosis of long COVID. Owing to a decline in the levels of COVID-specific antibodies, a negative serology test may not be a true indication of the absence of prior SARS-CoV-2 infection.

The diagnostic criteria by Raveendran play an important role in the confirmation of the diagnosis in the case of negative serologic testing and variability in the demonstration of COVID-related symptoms. The proposed diagnostic criteria comprise essential criteria, clinical criteria, and duration criteria. The "essential criteria" for the diagnosis of long COVID are based on the evidence regarding COVID within the duration of 2-4 weeks. It is further divided into symptomatic or asymptomatic confirmed, probable, possible, and doubtful cases. Further information about the Raveendran diagnostic criteria is given in the succeeding chapters.

Unlike other disorders, individuals with long COVID are not required to undergo extensive investigations and evaluations. The presenting symptoms determined the appropriate laboratory investigations. The clinical evaluation involves the documentation of both existing and new problems. Based on more conspicuous residual COVID symptoms, long COVID is categorized as post-COVID fatigue syndrome, post-COVID neuropsychiatric syndrome, post-COVID hepato-biliary syndrome, post-COVID thromboembolic syndrome, post-COVID dermatological syndrome, and post-COVID cardio-respiratory syndrome. This categorization facilitates the identification of the cause and assists in ruling out fatal complications of SARS-CoV-2 infection and long COVID.

The physician shall also assess the improvement of symptoms during each visit, along with documentation of all the related problems or symptoms of long COVID.

Treatment and Management of Long COVID

Treatment and management of long COVID involve a multidisciplinary approach. This includes clinical evaluation, treatment to provide symptomatic relief, the treatment of underlying pathologies, psychological support, physiotherapy, and occupational therapy. Cough suppressants, oral antibiotics, and paracetamol can be used for symptomatic treatment of minor symptoms such as cough, myalgia, and pain. Appropriate standard protocols are employed for the treatment of underlying pathologies associated with the symptoms. These etiologic factors may include pulmonary embolism, coronary artery disease, and cerebrovascular accident. Patients with neuromuscular and pulmonary complications may require neuro-rehabilitation and chest physiotherapy.

The treatment approach shall be optimized according to the requirements and the health status of the patient. Health conditions such as diabetes mellitus, cardiovascular diseases, and hypertension may exacerbate following SARS-CoV-2 infection. Therefore, the treatment and management modalities shall be optimized for patients with underlying comorbidities.

The nature, duration, and frequency of follow-up vary between patients. Individuals with critical health conditions are required to visit physicians more regularly and undergo laboratory investigations more frequently. However, patients who exhibit mild to moderate symptoms, which tend to improve over time, are required to visit physicians less frequently. Follow-up for such patients may take place via virtual consultations, limiting face-to-face interactions between patient and physician. On the contrary, individuals with acute worsening of existing symptoms or acute development of newer symptoms are recommended to visit the emergency department. (MS;Shaik, 2021)

Chapter 2 Useful Examinations for Long COVID

Introduction

A significant proportion of individuals who recovered from the SARS-CoV-2 infection demonstrate the persistence of symptoms as part of long COVID, a lingering outcome of SARS-CoV-2 infection. In order to carefully and effectively manage and treatment of patients with long COVID, it is important for physicians to correctly diagnose the condition and rule out other underlying etiologies. This chapter provides useful information regarding the challenges in the diagnosis, diagnostic criteria proposed by Raveendran, descriptions of clinical visits of patients with long COVID, clinical assessment tools and techniques according to each symptom, and differential diagnosis.

Challenges in the Diagnosis of Long COVID

The diagnosis of long COVID is relatively straightforward in patients who present with a history of COVID-related symptoms, the persistence of symptoms over a long duration, and a positive PCR test of the throat swab. However, patients presenting with persistent COVID symptoms over a long duration and a negative PCR test of the throat swab have a challenging evaluation and diagnosis in routine clinical practice. A significant percentage of long haulers are asymptomatic during the period of infection. The occurrence of COVID-related symptoms in these individuals following recovery from the infection contributes to the diagnostic challenges. The duration of the onset and persistence of symptoms also varies from patient to patient. This also adds to the diagnostic challenges regarding the differentiation of acute COVID and long COVID.

The following criteria are proposed to counter the challenges in the diagnosis of long COVID and make an accurate and prompt diagnosis in clinical settings. The criteria may also help individuals in reaching a diagnosis on their own.

Raveendran's Diagnostic Criteria for Long COVID

Raveendran's diagnostic criteria for long COVID comprises essential criteria, duration criteria, and clinical criteria. The "essential criteria" pertains to the evidence regarding the onset of prior SARS-CoV-2 infection, whereas the "clinical criteria" describe the symptoms associated with long COVID. Using these criteria, Raveendran has classified long COVID into doubtful, probable, possible, and confirmed long COVID.

The diagnostic essential criteria in symptomatic patients are as follows.

1. In "confirmed cases" of long COVID, the patient presents with clinical features associated with COVID-19 and a positive PCR test of the throat swab. (OR) The patient presents with clinical features associated with COVID-19, a negative PCR test of the throat swab, and a positive antibody test.

2. In "probable cases" of long COVID, the patient presents with clinical features associated with COVID-19, negative PCR test of throat swab, negative antibody test, contact with infected individuals within the duration of 2 weeks of development of symptoms, and chest x-ray or CT thorax findings consistent with SARS-CoV-2 infection. (OR) The patient presents with clinical features associated with COVID-19, negative PCR test of throat swab, negative antibody test, contact with infected individuals within the duration of 2 weeks of development of symptoms, and lack of relevant chest x-ray or CT thorax findings.

3. In "possible cases" of long COVID, the patient presents with clinical features associated with COVID-19, negative PCR

test of throat swab, negative antibody test, chest x-ray or CT thorax findings consistent with SARS-CoV-2 infection, lack of evidence regarding contact with infected individuals within the duration of 2 weeks of development of symptoms, and community transmission of the SARS-CoV-2 infection. (OR) Patient presents with clinical features associated with COVID-19, negative PCR test of throat swab, negative antibody test, lack of relevant chest x-ray or CT thorax findings, lack of evidence regarding contact with infected individuals within the duration of 2 weeks of development of symptoms, and community transmission of the SARS-CoV-2 infection.

4. In "doubtful cases" of long COVID, the patient presents with clinical features associated with COVID-19, negative PCR test of throat swab, negative antibody test, lack of relevant chest x-ray or CT thorax findings, lack of evidence regarding contact with infected individuals within the duration of 2 weeks of development of symptoms, and absence of transmission of SARS-CoV-2 infection in the community.

The diagnostic essential criteria for asymptomatic patients are as follows.

1. In "confirmed cases" of long COVID, the patient may either have a positive antibody test or positive PCR test of throat swab, or both.
2. In "probable cases" of long COVID, the patient has negative antibody test, negative PCR test of throat swab, negative findings on thorax CT, contact with infected individuals, and chest x-ray findings consistent with SARS-CoV-2 infection.
3. In "possible cases" of long COVID, the patient has a negative antibody test, negative PCR test of throat swab, lack of relevant chest x-ray or CT thorax findings, and contact with

infected individuals.

4. In "doubtful cases" of long COVID, the patient has a negative antibody test, negative PCR test of throat swab, lack of relevant chest x-ray or CT thorax findings, lack of evidence regarding contact with infected individuals, and community transmission of SARS-CoV-2 infection.

The clinical criteria pertain to symptoms associated with long COVID. These symptoms may be new or persistent and include fatigue, cough, muscle ache, joint pain, breathlessness, chest pain, and headache.

As indicated by its name, the duration criteria describe the nature of the disease in terms of the duration of symptoms. In symptomatic patients with long COVID, the mild disease is indicated by the presence of symptoms for longer than 2 weeks, moderate or severe disease is indicated by the presence of symptoms for longer than 4 weeks, and critical illness is indicated by the presence of symptoms for longer than 6 weeks. In asymptomatic patients with long COVID, the onset of symptoms following 2 weeks of positive PCR test, the onset of symptoms following 1 week of positive antibody test, or the onset of symptoms following 2 weeks of consistent chest x-ray or CT thorax findings are indicative of a diagnosis of long COVID.

Planning of Care – What Each Visit Looks Like?

The first visit of the patient to the primary care center involves a detailed medical history, physical examination, and laboratory evaluation for identifying the probable etiological factors associated with the symptoms of long COVID. The initial visit shall be made during the 4th week following the onset of COVID-related signs and symptoms or confirmation of the diagnosis. The healthcare staff shall obtain detailed information regarding the personal background of the patient, including the pre-infection status of the health of the patient. Complete data including complications associated with both infection and long COVID, the date of onset of symptoms and their duration, and admission in healthcare facilities including the intensive care unit (ICU) and the emergency department shall be recorded by the healthcare provider. (Aiyegbusi et al., 2021)

This is followed by a complete physical examination of the patient. This includes measurement of baseline oxygen saturation and vital signs of the patient. The healthcare provider shall also examine the cardiovascular system, respiratory system, and oropharynx of the patient. The diagnostic tests may vary from patient to patient according to the severity of the disease and the presenting signs and symptoms. Following is the list of all the diagnostic tests associated with the evaluation of patients with long COVID.

1. Vital signs
2. Electrocardiogram
3. Lung ultrasound
4. Chest x-ray
5. Oxygen saturation
6. Chest CT

7. Funduscopy
8. Spirometry
9. Abdominal ultrasound
10. Digestive endoscopy
11. Joint ultrasound
12. Fecal occult blood
13. Hemogram
14. D-Dimer
15. Sodium/potassium (Na/K)
16. C-reactive protein
17. Ferritin
18. Erythrocyte sedimentation rate
19. Liver profile
20. Thyroid function
21. Nutritional profile
22. Renal profile
23. Proteinogram
24. Pancreatic profile
25. Anti-transglutaminase antibodies
26. Natriuretic peptides
27. Complement
28. Rheumatoid factor
29. Antinuclear antibodies
30. Muscular enzymes
31. Serum cortisol

Chest ultrasound is a useful complementary test in primary care settings. In contrast to chest x-ray, it is accessible, efficient, and beneficial for the monitoring of health conditions. A chest ultrasound can demonstrate focal or diffuse pulmonary interstitial disease, pneumothorax, peripheral pulmonary involvement, pleural effusion, and thromboembolic or pneumonic pleural contact condensations.

The second visit of the patient with long COVID shall be made during the 8th week. During the visit, the healthcare provider assesses the outcomes of the tests conducted during the first visit, makes a differential diagnosis, and uses different diagnostic algorithms for recognizing the etiological factors associated with the symptoms of long COVID. The third visit is characterized by the evaluation of how the symptoms of long COVID have evolved during clinical visits. The healthcare provider also conducts a re-assessment of etiological factors associated with the symptoms. The third clinical visit shall be made from the 12th week of the occurrence of symptoms of confirmation of the diagnosis. (Ziauddeen et al., 2022)

Clinical Assessment based on Symptoms

1. Fatigue is an extra-respiratory symptom, which occurs at a frequency of 35-45%, 30-77%, and 16-55% 4 weeks, 8 weeks, and 12 weeks after the infection respectively. Concerning patients who present with fatigue, the healthcare provider shall investigate pre-infection diseases, organ-specific complications of long COVID, and symptoms accompanying fatigue. Laboratory evaluations shall include assessment of plasma cortisol levels, chloride, bicarbonate, phosphate, calcium, muscle enzymes, and spirometry.

2. Arthralgia or non-arthritic and non-inflammatory joint pain in one or more joints, persisting for longer than 4 weeks, is a symptom of long COVID. The clinical history shall include the date of origin of pain, location, duration, nature, response to analgesic therapy, and changes in the severity of pain with rest or movement. The healthcare provider shall also investigate the co-existing symptoms and previous disorders associated with arthralgia. The laboratory tests include proteinogram, uric acid, rheumatoid factor, antinuclear antibodies, and complement C3 and C4. In the case of suspected joint inflammation, joint ultrasound is performed.

3. Myalgia or muscle pain is a benign and self-limiting condition, which affects ≥ 1 muscle. Myalgia may also involve fascia, ligaments, and tendons. The persistence of myalgia for longer than 4 weeks following SARS-CoV-2 infection, requires specific diagnostic approaches. While obtaining the clinical history, the healthcare provider shall record the date of onset, duration, location, triggering factors, relieving factors, response to analgesic therapy, symptoms accompanying myalgia, and changes in the severity of myalgia with rest or movement. The laboratory tests including

antinuclear antibodies, aldolase, proteinogram, lactate dehydrogenase, creatine kinase, and rheumatoid factor may be useful.

4. Chest pain is a persistent symptom among patients with long COVID. Long haulers often report chest pain as high central chest pain or pulmonary burning. The healthcare provider shall obtain information regarding the date of development of the chest, duration, location, triggering factors, co-existing symptoms, prior history of trauma, and changes in chest pain with rest or movement. Further evaluation may include measurement of creatine phosphokinase and troponins, chest ultrasound, spirometry, and electrocardiogram.

5. Cough is also a common symptom observed in patients with long COVID. Individuals with cough persisting for greater than 4 weeks shall be approached by obtaining the clinical history and subsequent lab investigations. The clinical history shall comprise the date of development of cough, characteristics, organ-specific complications associated with coughing, and accompanying symptoms. Spirometry is recommended for patients presenting with this symptom.

6. Patients with long COVID may exhibit long-term dyspnea. During the initial clinical, the healthcare provider obtains information about the characteristics, date of onset, accompanying symptoms, organ-specific complications, and newer symptoms co-existing with shortness of breath. The laboratory investigations include creatine phosphokinase, troponin, and natriuretic peptides. CT, angio-CT, gasometry, respiratory functional tests, and chest radiology may also be considered.

7. Partial loss of smell (hyposmia) or complete loss of smell (anosmia), is yet another symptom long haulers exhibit. Loss of smell may also impair the ability of an individual to

discriminate between flavors, leading to loss of taste, known as ageusia or dysgeusia. The diagnostic approach for post-viral olfactory loss includes the acquisition of clinical history about the date of onset, comorbidities, and characteristics of the condition. This is followed by a complete otolaryngological exam and other suitable physical examinations.

8. The diagnostic approach for patients with long COVID, suffering from headaches for longer than 4 weeks following the SARS-CoV-2 infection, includes clinical history, physical examination, and neurological assessment. The clinical history includes data regarding the data of occurrence of symptoms, prior diagnosis of neurological diseases, and co-existing symptoms. The examination comprises inspection and palpation of the temporal artery in patients who are older than 50 years of age, assessment of blood pressure, examination of temporomandibular joint, and palpation of the cranium to identify triggers and sensitive points associated with the onset of headaches. The neurological assessment of patients with headaches includes dysmetria, facial asymmetry, gait, level of consciousness, funduscopy, Romberg test, and meningogenic signs.

9. The persistent digestive signs and symptoms in patients with long COVID include nausea, abdominal pain, diarrhea, and anorexia. Individuals with the persistence of these symptoms for longer than 4 weeks shall provide detailed clinical history regarding the characteristic features, date of onset, prior gastrointestinal disorders, and the associated therapies. The laboratory tests for digestive signs and symptoms include anti-transglutaminase, pancreatic enzymes, and tissue immunoglobulin A. The physician may also perform an abdominal ultrasound, food intolerance test, digestive

endoscopy, functional assessment, and evaluate fecal occult blood.

10. Long COVID can be regarded as a stressful event in an individual's life, which may result in temporary intense loss of hair, known as telogen effluvium. Other long-term symptoms include fever, chills, rhinitis, tinnitus, nasal congestion, intolerance to changes in the temperature, pain, vertigo, sleep disorders, oropharyngeal discomfort, concentration disorder, and conjunctivitis.

Differential Diagnosis

Examinations for long COVID must include strategies and necessary laboratory investigation to perform to enlist differential diagnoses and carefully rule out the pathologies that are not associated with SARS-CoV-2 infection or long COVID. In addition to this, the physicians must also identify prior pathologies or disorders in the medical record of the patient during primary care assessment. This is particularly useful as pre-existing health conditions may exacerbate during or following the SARS-CoV-2 infection. The physician may order the necessary tests to rule out different pathologies. The following conditions are considered in the differential diagnosis of long COVID.

1. Pulmonary embolism'
2. Postviral bacterial pneumonia
3. Ischemic heart disease
4. Lung fibrosis or atelectasis
5. Deep vein thrombosis
6. Post viral myocarditis
7. Arrhythmias
8. Myocardial scarring or fibrosis
9. Stroke
10. Congestive heart failure
11. Seizures
12. Anxiety
13. Cerebral vein thrombosis
14. Depression
15. Post-traumatic stress disorder
16. Insomnia
17. Bacterial, fungal, and other non-SARS-CoV-2 infections

Chapter 3 Therapy Options Available for Long COVID

Introduction

Patients with the diagnosis of long COVID require a holistic treatment approach, which is usually focused on the rehabilitation of the patient and self-management strategies. The holistic treatment approach shall be specifically tailored according to the requirements of the patient, the persisting signs and symptoms, the severity of signs and symptoms, and associated co-morbidities. In addition to symptomatic relief of the affected individuals, the treatment strategies also focus on managing and treating the etiological factors responsible for the onset of long COVID symptoms. In the case of acute onset of critical symptoms, it is recommended that the patients must report to the emergency department at their earliest. The patients must also be closely monitored for improvement or worsening of symptoms, as well as for modifying the treatment regimen according to the changing health status and patient's requirements over the course of the disease.

Pharmacological Approaches in the Treatment of Long COVID

Pharmacological interventions are an integral component of conventional therapeutic approaches toward the symptoms and underlying etiologies associated with long COVID. This section will discuss the role of potential medications in the pharmacological treatment of long COVID.

Long COVID is associated with the onset of chronic inflammation, demonstrated by an increase in the levels of proinflammatory cytokines. Anti-inflammatory drugs can be beneficial for alleviating the symptoms associated with long COVID, to some extent.

Viral-infected cells are subjected to oxidative stress. For instance, oxidative stress in the endothelial cells may lead to damage to the capillaries and result in local hypoxia. Nuclear factor erythroid 2-related factor 2 (NRF2) activator drugs can potentially enhance the expression of genes that encode antioxidant enzymes. Increased transcription of these enzymes leads to an increase in the levels of glutathione, which is an intracellular antioxidant. (Castanares-Zapatero et al., 2022)

Melatonin is a useful drug that modulates the NRF2 pathway as well as performs other useful functions. The functions include immunomodulation, neuroprotection, anti-oxidative function, cardioprotection, anti-inflammatory function, modulation of the cardiac rhythm, antineoplastic properties, fixation of sleep dysfunction, regulation of metabolism, and control of the process of melanogenesis. Although melatonin has been demonstrated as a pharmacological intervention for acute SARS-CoV-2 infection, the drug plays a potential integral role in the treatment of long COVID. It is particularly useful for neuropsychiatric symptoms in patients with long

COVID. These symptoms may include insomnia, anxiety, and depression,

Melatonin hormone is famously regarded as the dark hormone, which promotes sleep and is released from the pineal gland during the night. The hormone is also synthesized and released by other tissues including bone marrow, placenta, retina, and gastrointestinal tract. Melatonin has a good safety profile when obtained orally. Melatonin along with its metabolite, 6-hydroxy metabolite, reduces organ damage, leads to a decline in the levels of an inflammatory cytokine interleukin 6 (IL-6), reduces oxidative stress, improves the function of the mitochondria, and activates nuclear factor kappa B (NFκB).

In addition to modulating inflammation, melatonin is also known to stimulate neurogenesis in the hippocampus of the brain, modulating the depressed behavioral state. This produces a neurobiological response that is coherent with the response produced by clinically effective antidepressant medications.

Atorvastatin and apixaban are other pharmacological formulations, which are potentially effective in the treatment of long COVID. Apixaban is a prophylactic anticoagulant that is used for venous thromboembolism. Atorvastatin attributes to its pleiotropic actions, which enable this drug to reduce vascular inflammation and oxidative stress, leading to improvement in endothelial function. These drugs are potentially beneficial in patients with long COVID as this disease is associated with a higher risk for damage to endothelium and thromboembolism.

What is the Role of Vaccines against SARS-CoV-2 in the Treatment of Long COVID?

While Western populations have been administered vaccines adequately, populations in the middle and low-income countries fail to receive adequate vaccination therapies. The vaccines play an integral role in protecting individuals against SARS-CoV-2 infection and subsequent COVID-19 disease, hence, also have a significant impact on the onset and progression of long COVID. In addition to vaccines against SARS-CoV-2, boosters, and social distancing are also important constituents of intervention against the onset of long COVID. As compared to the prevention of SARS-CoV-2 infection, vaccines play a much greater role in reducing the severity and improving survival associated with SARS-CoV-2 infection. The protective effect of vaccines can be influenced by the variant under consideration, reinfection with the virus, and the current existence of long COVID in individuals receiving the vaccine and/or booster shots. A theoretical risk also implies that vaccines may exacerbate and or are responsible for the onset of symptoms similar to those of long COVID. A study investigated the outcomes of vaccination and demonstrated that 31% of participants had worsening symptoms, 22% of participants showed improvement in the symptoms, whereas 47% of participants demonstrated no changes in the symptoms after receiving the vaccine.

How does Treatment of Acute COVID Influence the Onset of Long COVID?

Owing to an increased health burden of long COVID, it is imperative to develop appropriate pharmacological interventions for the treatment and management of patients with long COVID. While vaccines play an important role in the protection of individuals against the infection, reducing the severity of the infection, and preventing the onset of long COVID in the vaccine recipients, medications may also be required for appropriate and effective patient management of long COVID.

An Italian study has demonstrated that the administration of remdesivir while the patient is hospitalized for the complaint of acute COVID, is beneficial for the prevention of the onset of long COVID in up to 33% of the cases. This medication must be administered in the form of an injection, owing to which it can't be utilized in non-hospital or non-clinical settings on a large scale. Other anti-viral drugs associated with the treatment of acute COVID, include molnupiravir and ritonavir or nirmatrelvir. These drugs are administered orally, are relatively less expensive, and function as protease inhibitors. These drugs introduce genetic mutations in the genome of the SARS-CoV-2, and are potential therapeutic strategies for combating the onset of long COVID in patients receiving these anti-viral medications.

Owing to the absence of viral persistence during long COVID, the anti-viral medications may not have a direct influence on the development and symptoms of long COVID. Corticosteroids including prednisolone and dexamethasone may be effective in dysgeusia, a symptom demonstrated by patients with long COVID, with olfactory training. However, otherwise healthy individuals are recommended against the use of corticosteroids due to associated health risks.

Hyperbaric Oxygen Therapy for Patients with Long COVID

Hyperbaric oxygen therapy is yet another useful strategy for the treatment of long COVID. In hyperbaric oxygen therapy, the patient breathes approximately 100% oxygen intermittently and is placed inside a hyperbaric chamber, which has a pressure greater than that of sea level. This therapeutic intervention is useful for both emergency medical conditions and elective conditions. The studies have demonstrated the safety and efficacy of hyperbaric oxygen therapy in the treatment and management of chronic fatigue syndrome. Fatigue associated with the onset of long COVID leads to the inability to work, participate in routine activities, engage with friends and family members, and perform physical activities. Hyperbaric oxygen therapy is beneficial for the management of symptoms in patients with long COVID. Patients subjected to this therapeutic intervention demand straight improvement in cognitive function and the overall fatigue score. This intervention has positive effects on neurologic symptoms, including brain fog and fatigue. The patients also report the transformation of their lives after undergoing hyperbaric oxygen therapy. Patients who received hyperbaric oxygen therapy for the management of COVID-related symptoms, do not report any adverse events, both during and after the treatment.

The Role of Cognitive Behavioral Therapy in the Treatment and Management of Patients with Long COVID

The rehabilitation clinics offer cognitive behavioral therapy for effective treatment and management of symptoms of long COVID, as well as post-viral fatigue syndrome. Cognitive behavioral therapy is effective for alleviating psychological symptoms associated with the onset of long COVID. The post-COVID stress response comprises fatigue, low-energy levels, palpitations, breathlessness, dizziness, discomfort, physical pain, hypervigilance, anxiety, depression, suicidal feelings, avoidance behavior, flashbacks, insomnia, and dissociation. Cognitive behavioral therapy is also a useful intervention for patients who are suffering from post-traumatic stress disorder, associated with intensive care admission owing to COVID-19. Cognitive behavioral therapy is defective for patients with long COVID, who are experiencing sleep problems such as insomnia. Quarantine and home confinement in such individuals may also lead to the onset of these sleep problems. CBT interventions can alleviate sleep problems among long COVID patients and promote better sleep practices. (Chen et al., 2022)

Integrative Approach to the Treatment of Long COVID

The onset of long COVID tends to impact the spiritual, social, physical, behavioral, and mental health of the affected individuals. Therefore, it is required by health care providers to opt for a multidisciplinary approach to treating patients with long COVID. Integrative help comprises conventional medicine, self-care strategies, and non-pharmacological approaches. Strategies that are relatively more effective than pharmacological interventions include exercises for depression, an anti-inflammatory diet for reducing inflammation associated with chronic conditions, and practicing mindfulness for the management of anxiety and stress. In addition to these strategies, the treatment plan also comprises yoga, meditation, journaling, and guided imagery. Not only do breathing exercises help in the management of anxiety and stress, but these exercises are also effective in the improvement of breathlessness in patients with long COVID. A comprehensive and coordinated approach toward the treatment and management of patients with long COVID helps improve the quality of life, quality of care, and overall well-being, and reduces the symptoms associated with long periods.

Psychological Interventions and Long COVID

The establishment of the pandemic related to acute infections followed by the development of long COVID, characterized by the persistence of symptoms and the onset of newer symptoms, poses a tremendous toll on the psychological health and well-being of the affected individuals, including children, adolescents, adults, and the health care providers. In addition to this, home confinement, limited social interaction, and restricted communication also contribute to the psychological effects of COVID. The psychological interventions may include active and passive telephone psychological counseling, one-to-one psychological crisis intervention, and self-adjustment of the patients. These psychological intervention models are effective in the management of sleep problems, anxiety, and depression in patients suffering from the symptoms of long COVID.

In addition to providing mental health support to patients with long COVID, for the management of suicidal ideation, post-traumatic stress disorder, anxiety, and depression, it is also important for the health care providers to ensure that the mental health services are easily accessible by the patients. The health care providers also play an important role in the identification of patients who require extra support and refer such patients to specialists for optimal management. Owing to the persistence of symptoms in long COVID, the patients may remain absent from work and require financial support from the government or other supporting bodies. The provision of social services support is helpful for patients who live alone and are subjected to stigma stigmatization or social isolation.

Physical, occupational, and speech therapists play an important role in the restoration of previous abilities of patients with long COVID.

In addition to this, the psychologist assists the patients in establishing a normal pattern for their diet, living style, sleep, and interpersonal relationships with peers, friends, and family members. The recovery of patients with long COVID is incomplete without adopting a holistic approach to the treatment and management of such patients, rather than focusing entirely on the elimination of the virus and providing symptomatic relief. Psychologists may also play an important role in filling memory gaps of patience with long COVID who suffered from significant memory loss during the disease. A holistic approach to the treatment and management of long COVID provides both mind and body with the required tools to recover completely and reach a normal state. Psychological interventions and mental health support are highly important in patients with long COVID, owing to the increased burden of mental illnesses among these individuals. In addition to psychologists, friends, family members, and peers may also play an important role in filling the blank spaces in memory and improving the mental, physical, and emotional well-being of the patient.

At certain times, the physicians may disregard the symptoms and clinical complaints of patients with long COVID, leading these patients to believe that their debilitating health condition is nothing but mere perception. This denial in the medical system leads to the demonstration of avoidance behavior of patients with long COVID, as they deviate from attaining medical attention and quality care. This leads to the worsening of symptoms associated with long COVID and adds to the suffering of patients, both on physical and psychological levels.

Chapter 4 Self-Management for Long COVID

Introduction

Individuals suffering from long COVID experience symptoms over a long duration. These symptoms include neurocognitive difficulties, fatigue, and breathlessness to name a few. Under usual circumstances, the clinical practice is largely focused on the management of symptoms. Individuals with acute COVID and long COVID may use self-prescribed medications for the management of symptoms. These medications include vitamin C, penicillin, antiretroviral medications, hydroxychloroquine and chloroquine, and traditional medications. While self-prescribing practices are relatively common among patients with COVID, these practices are associated with higher mortality rates from COVID-19. Self-prescription practices are also associated with limited access to healthcare services during the pandemic and due to a lack of adequate preventive and treatment approaches for COVID-19. This chapter discusses the importance of self-management strategies in patients with long COVID and describes the role of self-management strategies in alleviating symptoms and improving the quality of life in these individuals.

Management of Breathlessness

Breathlessness is an important and common symptom seen in individuals with long COVID. These individuals require pulmonary rehabilitation for reducing breathlessness and improving their quality of life. Loss of strength and fitness while the disease may also cause the patients to become breathless easily. Breathlessness can make an individual feel anxious, which leads to the worsening of breathlessness. The patients can opt for certain positions to reduce breathlessness and increase calm breathing. One technique requires an individual to lie flat on his or her stomach in a prone position. This may be a useful position for reducing breathlessness. Breathlessness can also be reduced by another position known as high side lying. This position requires the individual to lie on his or her side, propped up by a few pillows, which support the head and neck. The patient is also required to bend his or her knees in this position. Other techniques include forward-leaning sitting with the arms of the patient resting on a table, forward lean setting without a table in front of the arms of the patient on the armrest or his or her lap, forward lean standing, and standing with back support with feet approximately 30 centimeters away from the supporting wall. (Lopez-Leon et al., 2021)

In addition to breathing positions, breathing techniques are also useful for the management of breathlessness. The first technique is called controlled breathing, which allows the patient to relax and control his or her breathing. This technique requires the patient to sit in a comfortable position and place one hand on his or her chest and one hand on the stomach. The patient then closes his or her eyes and starts focusing on breathing. The patient must slowly breathe in through the nose and breathe out through the mouth. As a person breathes, he or she feels the stomach rising greater than the chest. Another technique is known as spaced breathing, which is useful in circumstances where the patient is carrying out activities with physical exertion. before initiating the physical activity, the patient must break down the activity into smaller components so that the patient does not end up becoming tired or breathless. Before making the effort, the patient must breathe in. The patient must breathe out when he or she is making the effort.

Physical Activity and Exercise

Long-term home confinement or hospitalization in patients with long COVID can significantly affect muscle endurance and strength. Exercise and increased physical activity are important for the restoration of muscle endurance and strength, alongside the management of the remaining symptoms of long COVID. During the initial stages, the patient may experience worsened fatigue and exacerbation of other symptoms associated with long COVID. This condition is described as post-exertional malaise. Recovery from this condition takes approximately 24 hours and may affect concentration, memory, energy levels, sleep, and elicit flu-like symptoms, joint pain, and muscle pain. Individuals suffering from this condition must avoid physical activities or exercises that triggered post-exertional malaise to conserve energy. Patients who do not experience this condition must increase the level of exercise or physical activity gradually to improve their levels of fitness, muscle endurance, and strength. Following are the stages of exercise that individuals can refer to while performing exercise at home.

1. Before jumping on to exercise techniques, an individual must prepare herself or himself for the exercise. Preparatory activities include gentle walking, balance exercises, stretching, and controlled breathing exercises. The patient may stretch muscles while standing or sitting. the stretch must be performed gently and one shall hold each stretch for approximately 15 to 20 seconds.

2. The next step is to perform the low-intensity activity. Examples of low-intensity activity include gardening tasks, light household tasks, or walking. The patient must remain in this phase without developing post-exertional malaise, to progress into the next phase of physical activity.

3. The next phase or phase three refers to moderate intensity activity. This includes jogging, resistance exercises, climbing up and down the stairs, the introduction of inclines, and brisk walking.
4. If the patient does not develop post-exertional malaise following phase three of exercises during a period of one week, he or she must progress to phase four of exercises pertaining to moderate-intensity physical activities. These activities are also associated with the development of functioning and coordination skills. The physical activities included in moderate-intensity exercises are dance classes, swimming classes, running, and cycling.
5. As an individual progresses to phase five of recommended physical activities, he or she can perform pre-COVID exercises, sports activities, and other physical activities.

Exercises to strengthen the muscles of arms include wall push-off, arm raises to the side, and bicep curl. Moreover, exercises to strengthen the muscles of the legs include sit to stand, heel raises, knee straightening, and squats. If the patient experiences pain while performing the above-mentioned exercises or physical activities, he or she must stop immediately and consult a healthcare professional before resuming the exercise program. (Lopez-Leon et al., 2021)

Strategies for Fatigue Management and Energy Conservation

Fatigue and low-energy levels are among the common debilitating symptoms associated with long COVID. The patients experience mental, cognitive, and physical fatigue during the disease. Following are some useful strategies an individual can adapt to reduce fatigue and improve functioning in routine life activities.

1. The first strategy is referred to as pacing. This strategy allows the individuals to manage their activities without exacerbating symptoms and developing post-exertional malaise. Before starting an activity, an individual must develop an activity plan, that is flexible and coherent with the current capabilities of that individual. As the symptoms and energy levels improve over time, an individual can increase his or her levels of activity in a controlled manner. Pacing ensures that the self-demands are exerted in a controlled manner, are coherent with the current capabilities of an individual, and are useful for the recovery of the individual.

2. Another useful strategy is known as prioritization. When the energy levels of the patient are relatively low, he or she must choose tasks that are more important for spending his or her energy on. Prioritization is also useful for it the recognition of activities that are relatively more important. Prioritization also enables an individual to identify activities that can be done with or without the assistance of a second individual.

3. The third strategy for fatigue management and energy conservation is known as planning. During planning activities, an individual shall spread out activities instead of fitting them in a single day. One shall complete high-energy tasks when the energy levels are relatively high. This can be

done when an individual grades his or her activities while planning them. In addition to planning activities, one shall also plan relaxation times to recharge for the upcoming activities. While suffering from long COVID and during the recovery, an individual must allow himself and herself plenty of rest during the day.

Management of Persistent Cough and Distorted Voice

Irritable cough, pooling of mucus in the throat, and sore throat associated with the onset of SARS-CoV-2 infection may lead to distortion of voice, resulting in a hoarse, weak, or breathy voice. Individuals who have had a breathing tube while their stay in hospital are more likely to experience problems with their voice. The following strategies are useful for combating these problems and improving the voice.

1. Affected individuals must practice good hydration and drink water throughout the day for a better voice.
2. Affected individuals must try not to whisper since whispering strains vocal cords. Such individuals must also avoid shouting and raising their voices.
3. Steam inhalation for a duration of 10 to 15 minutes facilitates moisturization of the vocal tract and combats dryness.
4. One must avoid eating foods associated with indigestion or consuming meals late at night to reduce the onset of gastric reflux.
5. Patients with long COVID shall also stop smoking.
6. If talking is uncomfortable or difficult for a patient, he or she must use other ways of communication, including gestures, writing, or texting.

Individuals with persistent and irritable coughs must follow the strategies enlisted below.

1. One must avoid breathing through the mouth and try breathing through the nasal passage.

2. Affected individuals shall practice the stop cough exercise. As soon as an individual senses the urge to cough, that individual shall shut his or his mouth and cover it with a hand. Simultaneously, the individual shall swallow and stop breathing. After suppressing the cough, an individual must begin breathing softly via his or her nose.
3. If the cough is associated with gastric reflux, an individual must lie on his or her side while sleeping or use a few pillows to prop herself or himself higher.

Management of Swallowing Difficulties

Owing to the weakness of muscles that facilitate swallowing, patients with long COVID may experience difficulties while swallowing drinks and foods. Individuals who have had breathing tubes during hospitalization, experience swelling and bruising of the throat, which leads to swallowing difficulties. The following techniques are useful for the management of the following problems.

1. One must always sit upright while consuming solid or liquid. An individual must not consume food while lying down.
2. After consumption of a meal, one must remain upright for at least 30 minutes. The individual may walk, stand, or remain seated.
3. In the initial stages, an individual must consume moist, soft, or smooth textured foods to assist swallowing. Later on, an individual may consume hard textured solid foods by chopping them into smaller pieces. One must not rush while eating and chew his or her food.
4. One must avoid talking during the consumption of a meal or a drink. Talking may lead to the opening of the airway, which causes the food to enter the airway and cause choking.
5. Individuals may get tired of eating full meals at a time. To tackle this problem, one must eat smaller portions during the day.
6. One must follow dental hygiene practices and remain hydrated throughout the day.

Management of Smell and Taste Problems

Patients with long COVID may complain of loss or reduced sensation of smell and taste. Following are some of the recommendations that an individual can adapt to combat these problems.

1. An individual must maintain good oral hygiene and brush his or her teeth twice a day.
2. An individual may perform olfactory or smell training twice a day. Olfactory training requires an individual to sniff certain smells such as eucalyptus, clove, lemon and rose for a duration of 20 seconds per substance.
3. For combating taste problems, one may incorporate fresh herbs, lemon juice, chili, and other herbs and spices to flavor his or her food. However, one must be cautious while using spices, as excessive spices may lead to the development or exacerbation of gastric reflux.

Management of Problems Associated with Thought Processes, Attention, and Memory

During long COVID and recovery from the viral infection, an individual may experience cognitive difficulties, memory loss, and problems pertaining to focus and attention. Cognitive problems or brain fog are exaggerated in the presence of fatigue. Tiredness and lower energy levels may impair the thinking skills of an individual. Before initiating strategies and techniques for improving cognitive problems, it is important for an individual to recognize the presence and severity of these problems. The following strategies are effective in reducing cognitive difficulties, improving attention, and thought processes.

1. An individual may work in a quiet place without any background distractions. In case of distractions, one may use air plugs when required. In case of visual distractions during reading, an individual can hide the text using paper or a finger.

2. Since fatigue exacerbate cognitive difficulties, attention problems, and impairment of thought processes, one may take frequent breaks and divide tasks into smaller components for the management of fatigue.

3. To complete a task successfully and remain motivated throughout the process, one shall break down the task into achievable goals. Completion of goals may further add to the motivation and improve the symptoms of patients with long COVID.

4. For tasks that require the application of thinking and cognitive skills, an individual shall plan these tasks when the energy levels are relatively higher.

5. An individual shall plan activities ahead of time by creating a schedule.
6. One must set rewards or incentives for himself or herself upon completion of a task or goal. The rewards range from drinking a cup of coffee to watching an interesting movie with the favorite snacks.
7. An individual must avoid rushing through the tasks as well as avoid the acquisition of information all at once. This may add to the fatigue and increases the chances of mistakes. One must deal with one task at a given time and progress to the next one after the completion of the previous task.
8. It becomes easier to keep a track of things when they are listed down in a calendar, diary or sticky note. Similarly, individuals who experience memory loss or tend to lose track of things may use these tools to support their memory in routine activities.
9. Brain exercises are also useful for improving cognitive function. An individual must perform brain exercises that facilitate thinking and are achievable, yet challenging enough to enhance memory and cognition. One may increase the difficulty level gradually. In addition to brain and memory exercises, one may also indulge in word games, number games, puzzles, and hobbies associated with improved memory and cognitive function.

Relaxation Techniques for the Management of Stress, Depression, and Anxiety

Patients with long COVID undergo a stressful experience during the disease and the recovery period. These experiences have a profound impact on the mood of an individual and can lead to the onset of stress, depression, or anxiety in the affected individuals. Different relaxation techniques have been developed to combat stress and manage the symptoms of depression and anxiety in patients with long COVID. These techniques help conserve energy and promote recovery, while enabling an individual to improve mood and control anxiety. The grounding technique is a form of relaxation technique that requires the patient to take slow and gentle breaths and ask herself or himself 5 questions. (Cha & Baek, 2021) These questions include the following.

1. What is one thing that I can taste right now?
2. What are two things that I can smell right now?
3. What are the three things that I can hear right now?
4. What are the four things that I can feel right now?
5. What are the five things that I can see right now?

The patient must spend a minimum of 10 seconds on each question and deal with sensation add a given time. One must recognize that the symptoms of long COVID are interlinked, and worsening of one symptom may lead to the worsening of other symptoms. Similarly, improvement in one symptom sets off the cycle and leads to improvement in other symptoms.

Alternative relaxation techniques include mindfulness, baths, aromatherapy, yoga, music, visualization, guided therapy, meditation, and Tai Chi. One must remain socially connected and communicate with peers, friends, and family members to reduce stress, acquire social support, and improve overall well-being. In addition to this, one shall consume a healthy and well-balanced diet as well as adopt good sleep practices for accelerating recovery and alleviating symptoms associated with long COVID. (Meagher, 2022)

Management of Pain

Self-prescription and excessive use of analgesic medications are associated with adverse health effects and increased mortality rates in patients with long COVID. The pain reported by patients with long COVID may be localized such as headache, abdominal pain, chest pain, joint pain, and muscle pain, or maybe generalized. The persistent onset of pain has a profound impact on fatigue levels, concentration levels, ability to work, and sleep. The pain cycle associated with long COVID comprises the development of pain, subsequent sleep disturbances, fatigue, stress, and the onset of depression and anxiety which further aggravate pain. The following measures can be adapted by the patients for the management of pain at home.

1. Individuals suffering from generalized pain, muscle pain, or joint pain may consume non-prescription analgesics with meals. These analgesics include ibuprofen or paracetamol.
2. For patients who do not respond to non-prescription analgesics (ibuprofen or paracetamol), may consult health care professionals for prescription medications to manage the pain.
3. While obtaining medications for the management of pain, an individual must aim to make the pain more manageable so that he or she can engage in daily activities, sleep profoundly, and function more effectively.
4. Adequate sleep can also facilitate the management of pain symptoms. For individuals who complain of sleep problems associated with pain, the pain medications can be timed according to the sleeping schedule to improve the quality of sleep.
5. One may also practice meditation or listen to relaxing music to reduce the intensity of planes.

6. Gentle exercises can alleviate pain by stimulating the release of endorphins in the body.

7. One must avoid overexertion and excess engagement in physical activities as this may lead to post-exertional malaise, which adds to pain, functional disability, and poor quality of life. Instead of engaging in excessive physical activities, one must engage in physical activities based on energy levels and health status.

Another self-management therapeutic approach, that may also benefit clinical treatment, is to track the symptoms associated with long COVID. Not only does this helps the patients observe symptomatic improvement, but also facilitates the health care providers in offering optimal treatment to the patients. Symptom tracking shall include the list of symptoms, both new and persistent symptoms, the severity of the symptoms, the date of onset of symptoms, and the date of the resolution of symptoms if any. It may also include details about complications associated with long COVID and physical, functional, emotional, and cognitive impairments experienced by the patient. The patient must track these symptoms in a diary or a chart that is easily accessible by the patient on a daily basis. (Jarrott et al., 2022)

Chapter 5 The Role of Nutrition in Long COVID

Introduction

You are what you eat. Nutrients not only determine the structural and functional integrity of an individual with the metabolic process involves, but also play an important role in the function of the immune system to protect the body against harmful pathogens. Individuals who consume a diet with good nutrition value tend to recover more quickly from diseases and are better able to return to the new normal. Moreover, the severity and nature of symptoms may also differ among individuals who consume a good diet as compared to individuals who fail to consume food with good nutrition value. In addition to intake of medications, the performance of exercises, the adaptation of useful relaxation and breathing techniques, and utilization of psychological interventions, patients with long COVID must also bring about lifestyle adjustments related to their dietary intake. This is an integral part of the self-management approach to the treatment of long COVID, discussed in the preceding chapter. This chapter described the importance of nutrition in the management and treatment of long COVID, as well as elaborates on the dietary components useful for individuals suffering from long COVID.

Importance of Nutrition in Treatment and Management of Long COVID

Sufficient consumption of fibers, fruits, vegetables, legumes, nuts, herbs, whole grains, seeds, dairy products, and other animal-based products nourishes the body and replenishes its stores of important nutrients, both macronutrients, and micronutrients. On the contrary, a diet with higher levels of saturated fats, refined sugars, processed ingredients, cholesterols, and pro-inflammatory substances has negative health consequences. A healthy, well-balanced, and antioxidant diet is useful for improving clinical outcomes of long COVID as well as aiding in the management and reduction of associated symptoms. (Raveendran et al., 2021)

Antioxidants, Polyphenols, and Long COVID

Antioxidants and polyphenols are important constituents of a plant-based diet. The substances affect blood flow towards the brain and enhance energy metabolism, as well as involved in cognition. Naturally occurring polyphenols are present in the plums, cherries, apples, tea, and onions. Even in low doses, polyphenols are known to demonstrate antidepressant properties, which may prevent or delay the onset of depression and anxiety. Quercetin is a polyphenol compound that works by inhibiting the enzyme, monoamine oxidase, thus, preventing the degradation of norepinephrine, dopamine, and epinephrine. This helps reduce the demonstration of depressive behavior. Quercetin also exhibits antiviral properties. Patients with long COVID may consume fruits and vegetables enriched in polyphenols to reduce, prevent, or delay the onset of depression and anxiety symptoms.

Fatty Acids and Long COVID

Fatty acids also play an important role in modulating the mental health of patients with long COVID. A beneficial nutritional approach to promoting mental health involved supplementation or dietary consumption of omega-3 essential fatty acids. These fatty acids demonstrate immunomodulatory and anti-inflammatory properties. A higher index of omega-3 fatty acids in the body is associated with lower rates of COVID-related mortality. Patients with critical SARS-CoV-2 infection demonstrated improvement in the renal and respiratory functional parameters with omega-3 fatty acids. Omega-3 fatty acids also improve the psychological resilience of individuals. Reduced intake of fatty acids associated with the production of pro-inflammatory mediators such as omega-6 fatty acids and increased consumption of omega-3 fatty acids have shown improvement in depression.

While plant-based diets exhibit favorable fatty acid ratios, animal-based food and processed food products have a greater ratio between omega-6 and omega-3 fatty acids. Therefore, the consumption of plant-based anti-inflammatory can facilitate the management of symptoms associated with inflammation as well as treat depression in patients with long COVID.

Diet and Quality of Sleep in Long COVID

Diet rich in an amino acid called tryptophan is associated with improved quality of sleep and alleviates sleep-associated problems in patients with long COVID in quarantine or home confinement. Diets high in fiber and low in saturated fat, such as plant-based products, promote better sleep, whereas increased levels of saturated fat and decreased content of fibers in the diet lead to less restorative and lighter sleep. Increased intake of magnesium is useful in the management of mental and physical stress in patients with long COVID. Good quality of sleep as a result of an appropriate diet, in turn, leads to a decrease in the symptoms of fatigue, low-energy levels, mood disturbances, depression, stress, and anxiety.

The Role of Diet in the Immune Response

Dietary components also affect the inflammatory biomarkers as well as the status of the immune system of an individual. Increased consumption of certain nutrients, as well as phytochemicals, are important for the modulation of the immune system. A vegan or plant-based diet demonstrates the mentioned characteristics and is useful for it influencing the immune response in patients with long COVID. Despite the inability of a plant-based diet in preventing the onset of acute and long COVID, this diet is effective in reducing the severity of the disease. The plant-based diet is enriched with polyphenols, phytosterols, and antioxidants, and has a positive influence on the cells associated with the immune function of the body. These chemicals also exhibit antiviral properties, hence are effective against the SARS-CoV-2 infection. Fat-soluble vitamins (vitamins A, E, and D), water-soluble vitamins, and polyphenols present in fruits, vegetables, and mushrooms improve the activity and functionality of natural killer cells. (Rajan, 2021)

Diet and Improvement in Musculoskeletal Pain Associated with Long COVID

Muscle pain, and joint pain, cumulatively known as musculoskeletal pain, are important symptoms in patients with long COVID. Not only these symptoms are responsible for the G debilitating nature of the disease, but are also associated with disability and lack of adequate functioning in the selected individuals. These symptoms persist during long COVID and are among the physical symptoms associated with long COVID that require prompt treatment and management. Musculoskeletal pain may impair the quality and duration of sleep in patients with long COVID, therefore, musculoskeletal pain also influences the symptoms of fatigue, depression, stress, anxiety, tiredness, and low-energy levels indirectly. In addition to prescription and nonprescription analgesic medications, nutrition also plays an important role in alleviating musculoskeletal pain and preventing its onset in patients with long COVID. Increased severity of musculoskeletal pain is associated with higher intake of fat and sugars, and lesser intake of fibers and fruit. Lower levels of folic acid and magnesium in the body also contribute to the chronic onset and severity of musculoskeletal pain.

Reducing consumption of animal-based products that have higher levels of saturated fatty acids and proinflammatory substances, and increased consumption of plant-based products that are rich in micronutrients, and fibers, and have lower levels of saturated fat, leads to improvement in both musculoskeletal pain and functionality of an individual. Alleviation of musculoskeletal pain also improves the quality of life in affected individuals. This sort of diet is also useful in individuals with chronic fibromyalgia symptoms, osteoarthritis, and rheumatoid arthritis. Higher levels of antioxidants in plant-based products help in the neutralization of free radicals, reduced exposure of the patient to pro-inflammatory substances, and maintenance of weight owing to lesser calorie density of a plant-based diet. The inflammatory pathways persist in patients who have recovered from SARS-CoV-2 to infection. This systemic inflammation is responsible for several symptoms demonstrated by patients with long COVID, including pain, and fatigue. Consumption of a healthy and well-balanced diet combats prolonged systemic inflammation present in patients with long COVID.

Dietary Recommendations for Patients with Long COVID

Individuals suffering from long COVID shall follow the dietary and nutritional recommendation listed below, to maintain health, alleviate symptoms, prevent complications, and accelerate recovery.

1. Individuals with long COVID struggle with low-energy levels and fatigue. It is recommended that patients with long COVID consume food rich in carbohydrates. Such foods are good sources of energy. Wholegrain foods have a lower glycemic index and release energy at a relatively slower rate. Pasta, potatoes, bread, and rice are foods containing greater concentrations of carbohydrates and provide higher levels of energy to patients with long COVID.

2. Since full portions of the meal are more likely to elicit tiredness in patients with long COVID, it is recommended that the meals are divided into relatively smaller portions that do not induce tiredness. The patient may consume meals in different forms—tinned, dried, fresh, or frozen.

3. In addition to foods rich in carbohydrates, the patients must also consume foods that are a rich source of proteins. These foods include pulses, nuts, seeds, eggs, meat, and fish. Processed meat such as sausages, bacon, burgers, and red meat must be consumed in moderation, as these food sources may contribute to the development of health complications. In comparison to a plant-based diet, animal-based foods comprise high levels of both saturated fats and pro-inflammatory markers. The presence of these markers contributes to chronic systemic inflammation observed in patients with long COVID. Hence, one must consume meat in moderation while consuming sufficient portions of plant-

based foods.

4. Individuals suffering from long COVID shall consume a diet rich in essential fatty acids, particularly omega-3 fatty acids. Plant-based sources that contain significant levels of omega-3 fatty acids include seeds, oils, soya, and nuts. Animal-based foods that are a rich source of omega-3 fatty acids, including sardines and salmon, can be consumed twice a week. One must ensure that the food patterns favor increased levels of omega-3 fatty acids in comparison with omega-6 fatty acids, as the latter is associated with increased synthesis of proinflammatory markers.

5. One must ensure that the diet contains greater quantities of unsaturated fat in comparison to saturated fat. However, fat in any form shall be consumed in moderation and according to the dietary requirements of the individual.

6. Dairy products including yogurt, milk, and cheese are a rich source of vitamins and proteins. In addition to this, dairy products are an important source of micronutrients, including calcium. Calcium is an essential mineral for keeping the bones healthy and improving the functionality and movement of patients with long COVID. In case an individual consumes dairy alternatives instead of dairy products, he or she must ensure that these daily alternatives are fortified with calcium to replenish the calcium stores in the body for optimal musculoskeletal health.

7. Hoarseness of voice, sore throat and irritation of the vocal tract are common occurrences in patients with long COVID. One must hydrate himself or herself regularly. Patients with long COVID shall consume plenty of fluids including milk, water, sugar-free drinks, smoothies, and fruit juices. Fluids containing both excessive natural or artificial sugars shall be either avoided or consumed in moderation.

8. For individuals who complain of loss of appetite or poor appetite, frequent consumption of smaller portions of easy snacks as well as nourishing drinks can provide energy and improve appetite. Individuals who experience loss of weight shall refer to their physician for identification of the underlying cause or prescription of nutritional drinks that can improve weight, energy levels, and appetite.

9. Dietary recommendations for individuals with complete or partial loss of taste and smell include the addition of strong flavors in their meals. In the case of failure to restore smell and taste sensation despite olfactory training and use of strong flavors in meal, the patient shall consult his or her physician for further work up.

10. Patients suffering from long COVID often complain of digestive symptoms including diarrhea, bloating, abdominal pain, and nausea. The persistence of these symptoms indicates the presence of different health conditions associated with the gastrointestinal tract, such as celiac disease and irritable bowel syndrome. Disruption of the gut microbiome may also elicit the occurrence of these symptoms. Plant-based foods including pulses, whole grains, nuts, seeds, fruits, vegetables, fiber, and seeds are useful for maintaining gut health and subsequently maintaining the composition of a healthy gut microbiome. The consumption of probiotics, both in the form of supplements and dietary constituents, can help restore the healthy composition of the gut microbiome. Concerning the gut-brain axis, psychological disturbances including sleep disorders, stress, anxiety, and depression may also influence the functioning and overall health of the gastrointestinal tract. These psychological symptoms may further exacerbate the gut symptoms, leading to a worsening of the overall health of

patients with COVID-19. In addition to dietary interventions, psychological interventions are also useful for alleviating gut symptoms and promoting gut health.

The Importance of Vitamin and Mineral Supplements in Long COVID

Patients with long COVID may demonstrate low levels of important micronutrients, vitamins, and minerals, in the body. These vitamins and minerals are important for optimal functioning of the body, regulation of important body processes, and strengthening the immune system of the body to fight off harmful pathogens. Low levels of such micronutrients in the body, in addition to dietary deficiencies, often lead to an increase in the severity of symptoms of long COVID. Moreover, patients with long COVID, who remain in quarantine or home confinement, are subjected to the minimum or no exposure to sunlight. This may serve as an important risk factor for the development of vitamin D deficiency in these patients.

In contrast to this, some patients with long COVID may consume higher than required doses of vitamins and minerals including vitamin B3, vitamin D, quercetin, zinc, and vitamin C to alleviate the symptoms associated with long COVID. While higher doses of vitamins and minerals have no added benefits, this may lead to adverse health effects. The patients may consume mineral supplements and multivitamins according to physicians' recommendations or manufacturer's instructions present on the label.

Individuals with long COVID shall track the changes in weight and appetite, in addition to tracking the symptoms of long COVID in the form of a chart or diary entry, as discussed previously. The consumption of restrictive diets is discouraged in the case of long COVID, as these may lead to complications associated with dietary restrictions. One must eat regularly and focus largely on a wide array of plant-based food products. While processed meats, animal-based food products, sugary drinks, and unhealthy snacks may look tempting, these may hinder recovery and may even worsen the health condition in patients with long COVID. Planning meals ahead of time are also useful. The meal shall consist of nourishing and energy-boosting drinks, quick snacks, and small portions of meals throughout the day. (Umesh et al., 2022)

Chapter 6 The Role of Sleep in Long COVID

Introduction

While sleep may seem a trivial part of daily routine in an individual's life, it actually holds immense importance in the psychological, cognitive, physical, and emotional well-being of an individual. Good quality sleep promotes brain performance and the overall health of an individual. Individuals who are unable to sleep properly or do not get enough sleep are more likely to develop heart diseases, obesity, dementia, stroke, and other health conditions as compared to individuals who receive good quality sleep for sufficient duration. The three attributes of sleep include the quality, the quantity, and the schedule of sleep. Inconsistency or problems associated with any of these features can lead to the development of different health disorders.

Sleep Problems in Patients with Long COVID

Sleep disturbances of moderate to severe intensity are highly prevalent in individuals suffering from long COVID. The potential causes of sleep disturbances in these patients include the autoimmune response of the body to the viral infection and the onset of post-traumatic stress disorder in patients with long COVID. Patients suffering from generalized anxiety disorder are more vulnerable to sleep problems coexisting with long COVID, as compared to individuals without a generalized anxiety disorder. The rates of insomnia, a form of sleep disorder, are higher in patients with long COVID than in other infectious diseases such as flu and respiratory tract infections. Sleep disturbances in long COVID are also associated with the onset of chronic inflammation in these patients. It is also suggested that altered exposure of quarantined or home-confined patients to sunlight and subsequent alterations in the release of melatonin, also influenced the development of sleep disorders in patients with long COVID. (Daines et al., 2022)

Importance of Sleep in Long COVID

Sleep plays an important role in both the treatment and management of patients with long COVID. In addition to being important symptoms of long COVID, sleep disorders may exacerbate the severity and frequency of other symptoms of long COVID, setting off a vicious cycle leading to debilitating health conditions for affected individuals. Lack of adequate and good quality sleep or the presence of an improper sleep schedule leads to the onset of fatigue, anxiety, depression, and low-energy levels in patients with long COVID. Therefore, good quality sleep not only improves the functioning of an individual but also alleviates depression, low-energy levels, fatigue, anxiety, and stress associated with long COVID.

Recommendations for Sleeping Disorders in Long COVID

The following recommendations by experts can be adapted by patients with long COVID for the management of sleep problems at home. These recommendations are useful for accelerating recovery and enhancing the overall health and well-being of the affected individuals. In the case of worsening symptoms or lack of improvement in sleep problems and associated disorders, the patients may consult their health care provider for further treatment and management of health conditions.

1. One must go outdoors in the morning for regulating the internal biological clock. Individuals who cannot go outdoors, such as individuals who are in quarantine, critically ill, or are not convenient, can sit by the window in the morning. Exposure to sunlight helps the body adapt to the normal schedule and regulate the internal body processes accordingly. The establishment of a normal circadian rhythm is useful for the normal functioning of the body. This facilitates the treatment, management, and recovery in patients with long COVID.

2. Patients with long COVID shall reduce their screen time during the night, particularly before going to sleep. exposure to light emitted by screen devices, may affect the circadian rhythm of the body and disrupt the sleep schedule. Instead of using screen devices, one may practice meditation, listen to music or podcast, listen to an audiobook, or read a book before going to bed. Patients with long COVID and healthy individuals, in general, must practice these activities before going to bed and limit screen time during this.

3. One shall plan a sleep schedule and remain consistent with

this schedule throughout. Taking long naps during the day and falling asleep late at night may disrupt the circadian rhythm of the body and contribute to the development of sleep disorders. Therefore, it is recommended that patients with long COVID refrain from taking long or frequent naps during the day and try sleeping early during the night.

4. Melatonin is a hormone released by the pineal gland. Also known as a dark hormone, this hormone is important for the regulation of the sleep cycle. To regulate the sleep cycle and manage sleep disorders in patients with long COVID, melatonin hormone can be consumed in a standard dose, approximately three to five hours before falling asleep. This hormonal supplement may restore the normal levels of melatonin in the body and help manage sleep disorders in individuals suffering from long COVID.

5. In addition to other strategies for improving the quality, duration, and schedule of sleep in patients with COVID-19, it is also recommended that patients must not remain in bed for longer periods if they do not aim to sleep or are unable to sleep for a long duration. Such patients are encouraged to indulge in relaxing activities including meditation, reading, and deep breathing, which reduces stress and elicits the feeling of relaxation and calmness. Instead of abruptly reducing time spent in bed, one must gradually decrease this time by scheduling sleeping time later during the night or waking time earlier during the day.

6. In addition to the treatment of psychological disorders, cognitive behavioral therapy is also useful for the treatment of insomnia in patients with long COVID. This involves the utilization of relaxation techniques and scheduling of routine activities of patients with long COVID, to combat anxiety and manage sleep disorders, including insomnia.

7. Physical activities including regular participation in routine tasks or potentially beneficial for improving the quality, duration, and schedule of sleep. Working out in a gym or simply walking outdoor can help an individual sleep better.

8. As discussed in the preceding chapter, diet is also associated with the quality of sleep. A healthy and well-balanced diet promotes good quality sleep. An anti-inflammatory, healthy, and plant-based diet helps reduce stress, both physical and psychological, in patients with long COVID. One must limit the intake of both caffeine and alcohol, as these substances may disrupt the quality and quantity of sleep.

9. Individuals with long COVID are constantly or mostly confined to their homes, and have limited exposure to the outside world and interaction with their loved ones. Simple activities including changing bedsheets, making the bed, and fluffing pillows make an individual feel both happy and fresh. Patients with long COVID may also opt for modifying their bedroom setup and use different sleep accessories for making sleep are relaxing process. While modifying the setup of their bedroom or other spaces around the house, individuals must refrain from exerting themselves. To do so, one must break down the task into smaller components or take the help of their friends, family members, or peers while performing these tasks.

Chapter 7 Exercise and Tools to Promote Recovery in Long COVID

Importance of Rehabilitation in Patients with Long COVID

The onset of long COVID in patients recovering from SARS-CoV-2 infection is associated with impairment of structural and functional integrity of these patients. Both the symptoms and therapeutic interventions of long COVID have a profound impact on the quality of life and participation of affected individuals in routine activities. Rehabilitation techniques and services facilitate these patients in the restoration of structural and functional integrity, normalization of physical fitness, and improvement in their participation in routine activities. In addition to the establishment of rehabilitation programs in the light of the pandemic, rehabilitation exercises by the patients themselves can help treat and manage the symptoms in patients with long COVID. In the rehabilitation of individuals suffering from long COVID, occupational therapists and physiotherapists play an important role in speeding up recovery and enhancing the overall health of these individuals. (Al-Aly et al., 2022)

Occupational Therapy in the Rehabilitation of Long COVID

Chronic fatigue is a common and important symptom in patients with long COVID, represented by extreme tiredness which is not relieved upon rest or sleep. The affected individuals find it difficult to cope with routine life activities and maintain good social interactions. Chronic fatigue may also lead to an increase in the severity of other symptoms in long COVID. Individuals with long COVID and chronic fatigue tend to have lower levels of energy; however, they constantly push their bodies to work harder and exert themselves during the process. As the body loses energy, the ability of the body to fight off infections and recover from long COVID also declines. Occupational therapists are integral to the recovery as well as treatment and management of symptoms in patients with long COVID. The aim of occupational therapy is to restore the levels of energy and improving the overall well-being of the affected individuals by promoting good nutrition, good quality sleep, management of stress, and development of depressed skills by the patients. The goal of occupational therapy is to improve the function of affected individuals in the domains of education, friendships, work, and routine tasks.

Following are different occupational therapy techniques useful for individuals with long COVID. These techniques can be practiced at home, or individuals can be assisted by occupational therapists in learning these techniques.

1. Before the utilization of further techniques, techniques associated with rest must be established first. Important techniques include relaxation, meditation, restorative rest techniques, and deep rest skills shall be practiced by patients with long COVID. Adequate rest and relaxation switch off

the stress response and induce the body to enter a state of rest and digestion. By practicing these breathing and relaxation techniques in clinical settings, the patients may master their responses for promoting the recovery of long COVID.

2. Management of mind is another useful occupational therapy technique, which enables patients with long COVID to cope with low mood, stress, and anxiety. This helps in the management of chronic fatigue. Mindfulness practices such as self-compassion and acceptance are effective tools in the management of energy levels and the overall well-being of patients with long COVID.

3. Pacing is a useful strategy to combat chronic fatigue in patients with long COVID. The patients must stop the activity or task and take a rest before becoming exhausted. This helps individuals in replenishing energy levels and gradually increasing their ability to perform routine tasks.

4. Occupational therapy also emphasizes the role of nutrition in the treatment and management of symptoms in patients with long COVID. The affected individuals must consume regular, healthy, well-balanced, and nutrient-rich foods, that restore their levels of energy. While larger portions of the meal are hard to digest, require higher levels of energy, and may contribute to chronic fatigue. This can be managed by consuming frequent and small portions of meals, which are easily digested, require lesser levels of energy, and help recover from chronic fatigue while providing the body with the necessary nutrients.

5. In addition to improved nutrition, the patients may also receive a good quality of sleep. Good sleep hygiene comprises regular sleeping and waking times, in addition to regular yet short rest breaks during the day. However, one must avoid taking longer naps, as this may disrupt the sleep schedule.

6. Patients with long COVID are encouraged to participate in activities that they derive pleasure from and find those activities enjoyable. Indulging in such activities helps regulate mood and improve the overall well-being of an individual.

7. The patient must gradually increase participation in different tasks and activities, provided that the energy levels of the patient align with the respective activity. Affected individuals must initiate building when he or she is confident about pacing and rest breaks. At this stage, the patients must build activity through daily occupation rather than exercises. The activities must be built at a slower rate, and the increase shall occur once per week. Gradual activity building allows the body to gradually increase its tolerance as the energy reserves also improve. An individual must continue to take rest breaks while building activity, to ensure that he or she does not run out of energy or exerts himself or herself during the process of activity building.

8. Occupational therapists advise individuals suffering from long COVID to have a longer phased return to their work. To reduce the aggravation of symptoms with a return to work, the patients must build activity slowly and gradually, improve work tolerance, take sufficient rest breaks, and make appropriate adjustments in the routine. The persistence of chronic fatigue symptoms for longer than a period of 12 weeks is rather alarming, and the patients must be referred to specialists for further diagnosis, management, and treatment.

Physical Therapy in the Rehabilitation of Long COVID

In addition to occupational therapy approaches, physical therapy is also integral to the rehabilitation of patients with long COVID. The majority of the affected individuals either isolate themselves or are subject to home confinement. During this, the patients spend the majority of their time lying down or sitting. This adds to reduced muscle strength, the onset of musculoskeletal symptoms including arthralgia and myofascial pain, greater risk for the development of deep vein thrombosis, and increased exercise intolerance in patients with long COVID. Physical therapy strategies in these individuals comprise muscle strengthening exercises, stretching, balance training, and low-intensity aerobic exercises. The physical exercises facilitate the strengthening of the immune system and cardiovascular system of the body and improve the physiological parameters of the body. (van Kessel et al., 2021)

Patients with long COVID suffering from respiratory difficulties can also benefit from physical therapy approaches. Not only do physical therapists facilitate improvement in the respiratory function of affected individuals, but also determine the need for hospitalization based on oxygen saturation and dyspnea assessment. Secretion clearance techniques are useful for patients with cough and patients who find it difficult to expectorate sputum. Respiratory exercises are encouraged in patients with mild symptoms of long COVID to improve the prognosis of the disease and alleviate the symptoms to improve respiratory health. Rehabilitation with physical therapy promotes recovery of functional impairment as well as lung damage in patients who survive severe SARS-CoV-2 infection. In addition to pharmacological interventions, rehabilitation techniques are considered useful for the recovery of patients with long COVID, involving both physical therapists and occupational therapists.

Important Exercises in Long COVID

Several exercises have been developed in order for the management and treatment of symptoms in patients with long COVID. Deep breathing exercises are part of a group of interventions under the umbrella of the active cycle of breathing techniques. These techniques facilitate expectoration of the sputum from the respiratory tract and can be taught by physiotherapists. The exercises include breathing control, deep breathing exercises, and huffing which further comprises small-long half and big-short half. (The Lancet, 2021)

1. The first technique, breathing control, involves breathing through the nose, pursing of lips if an individual breathes through the mouth, relieving tension as an individual is breathing out, gradually increasing the duration of breaths, and closure of eyes to relax and increase focus on breathing. While performing other active exercises, breathing control can be practiced in between these exercises. Breathing control is also a useful strategy during times of panic or anxiousness.

2. The deep breathing exercise involves deep breaths through the nose while keeping both shoulders and chest relaxed. An individual may take three to five deep breaths at a time. Holding breath for approximately two to three seconds before breathing out is helpful for some individuals.

3. In contrast to other breathing techniques, huffing involves breathing out through the mouth and throat, facilitating the clearance of sputum in a controlled manner. each individual must practice breathing control after huffing. While a small-long huff helps clearance of sputum from lower aspects of the chest, a big-short huff facilitates the movement of sputum from higher aspects of the chest. These techniques promote the clearance of sputum from the respiratory tract without

coughing.

In addition to breathing exercises, there are different exercises available for improving the physical strength as well as the functioning of individuals suffering from long COVID. These exercises can be performed while the patient remains seated, to facilitate the strengthening of the muscles while preventing the patient from exerting himself or herself or developing post-exertional malaise. These exercises can be easily performed at home and are listed as follows. (Chandan et al., 2022)

1. "Seated-knee extension" requires an individual to sit upright and initiate the exercise with a bent knee. This is followed by lifting off the foot while straightening the knee. The patient may hold the leg for 10 seconds.
2. "Sit-to-stand" involves standing up and sitting down on the chair with the use of arms for support.
3. "Seated hip flexion" requires an individual to sit upright and keep both feet on the surface. While remaining seated, the patient is required to march his or her legs while alternating between right and left legs.
4. "Shoulder strengthening" required the patient to remain seated in an upright position with arms by the side. This is followed by lifting the arms to shoulder height and then back by the side. The patient may add weights, for instance, a tin of chickpeas.
5. "Bridging" requires a patient to lie on his or her back on the bed. The patient must squeeze the bottom and lift it off the bed.
6. "Straight leg raise" requires the patient to lie on his or her back on the bed. This is followed by keeping one leg straight and lifting the leg off the bed. This shall be repeated with both legs.

7. "Standing leg exercises" involve the patient standing with both feet together and using a firm chair for providing support. This is followed by lifting the outer leg to the side and then a slow return of the leg to the initial position. The exercise is repeated by the lifting the leg backward and lifting the knee in the forward direction.

Chapter 8 Navigating your Return to Work

Introduction

The recovery from long COVID is a tiring and lengthy process. This involves dietary improvements, physical activity, and the use of medications for the alleviation of symptoms as well as the prevention of relapse of the disease. Individuals who remain absent from work owing to long COVID may face several difficulties while rejoining and resuming their work. Such individuals may also be uncertain about their physical and mental potential, in coherence with returning to the work. They may potentially be confused about the time that they shall be joining their work and whether it will have negative consequences on their health. Moreover, their return to work is accompanied by joint efforts of the office team and the patients themselves in bringing about work adjustments. The following sections of this chapter elaborate on the common concerns of patients about navigating their return to their professional lives.

When to Return to Work?

There are various obstacles to returning to work among patients who are suffering from long COVID. Physicians play an important role in helping patients navigate obstacles and help them overcome these obstacles. For the patients to feel positive about going to work, the patients shall be encouraged to contact their office personnel about the potential work adjustments that can be made for the gradual return to work. While some long COVID patients experience alleviation of symptoms, they may experience the recurrent onset of symptoms and disease relapse. This may affect their work and even cause the patients to leave work at all. Prior discussion with the office personnel, such as the patient's line manager, is beneficial for work-related adjustments. The physician may assess the overall health of the patient and assure the patient about the management of symptoms and their health condition.

Individuals can plan their return to work when the symptoms are either improved over the course of time or have remained the same, when the individuals are capable of carrying out their routine activities without worsening their health condition, and when the individuals are capable of managing their symptoms.

Prerequisites for Returning to Work after Long COVID

Before the planning of return to work in patients with long COVID, the patients may assess themselves to see whether they are mentally and physically fit for returning to work. The patients may answer the following questions about assess their health and fitness?

1. Have you allotted specific time for rest?
2. Are you multitasking or managing multiple tasks at a given time?
3. Are you capable of carrying heavy loads?
4. Are you capable of working quickly?

The patient shall gradually increase his or her routine activities and track the time it takes to complete a task. This may also help the patient in discussing the return-to-work strategy with the office personnel. In addition to assessing the current health condition and tracking the duration of completion of tasks, the patient shall also focus on the progress related to recovery from long COVID. The patient shall track the recovery progress as well as identify any patterns present. Recovery from long COVID is characterized by the absence of an increase in the symptoms of long COVID, the symptoms shall not persist for more than a few hours, and the ability to continue with routine activities.

Work Adjustments

The potential workplace adjustments associated with the return to work of long COVID patients include the following. These workplace adjustments facilitate the process of recovery and make the return a safe and easy process for both the patient and the stakeholders.

1. Equipment including a special chair or desk to facilitate both working and comfort of the patient.
2. Provision of extra support to the patient while working.
3. Provision of time off to the patient to accommodate the medical appointments.
4. The working days for patients with long COVID shall be relatively shorter.
5. A ramp at the entrance of the building may be useful for the patient to enter the workplace.
6. The patient shall have different work patterns to accommodate their health requirements. The altered work patterns may have frequent breaks to promote rest and comfort for the patient.
7. The employer may help the patient in working from home in case the patient is unable to work in a professional setting.
8. The employer shall ensure that the cognitive, physical, and mental tasks allotted to the patient shall be less demanding.
9. The employer shall modify the workload. The work allotted to the patient shall comprise less complex or relatively fewer tasks. This is useful for the prevention of worsening the health condition of the patient recovering from long COVID.

The Role of Employers

The following strategies can be adapted by the employer to help patients with long COVID in adjusting to the work environment and recovering from the disease.

1. The employer shall engage in regular conversations with the employees to ensure their well-being of the employees.
2. The employer shall observe the employees and ensure that the employees are satisfied with the work adjustments.
3. The employer shall discuss work-related adjustments with the employees and make further adjustments if important.
4. The employer may also recommend peer networks and long COVID support groups to their employees. The employer may also offer psychological support and well-being services to the employees when required.
5. In case of absence from work, the employer shall keep in touch with the employee to offer support.
6. The employer may also offer the employees occupational health services to ensure proper recovery.
7. The employer shall assign tasks that are less mentally, emotionally, and physically demanding to the employees recovering from long COVID.
8. The employer may also allow the employees to return to the office on an extended or standard phase return.

What to do if you are Unable to Join at Work?

In case an individual is unable to return to work, the patient shall prepare himself or herself for returning to work later in the upcoming future. You can opt for other alternate activities to engage in work and remain up to date on the current proceedings at work. The following activities can be adapted when a person has delayed his or her return to work.

1. The patient with long COVID may attend virtual appointments in place of working directly in the office.
2. The patient may engage in at-home exercises while recovering from long COVID.
3. The patient may attend rehabilitation classes while recovering from long COVID.
4. The patient may monitor his or her symptoms by maintaining an activity diary.
5. The patient may the professional advice of an occupational health therapist or other healthcare practitioners.
6. The patient may also apply for welfare benefits associated with recovery from long COVID.

In case a patient does not feel ready to resume his or her work in a professional capacity, he or she shall talk to the team or line manager at the office. The patient may also consult the occupational health department at the office to make work-related adjustments.

Return to Work Guidelines

Following is a brief guideline about returning to work for patients who are suffering from long COVID.

1. Health professionals play an important role in providing advice about returning to work as soon as possible for the patient with long COVID.
2. The recommended practice is to establish contact with the employer within the initial two weeks of the onset of symptoms of long COVID and absence from the workplace.
3. The stakeholders including the employers and the healthcare professionals shall be actively involved in the integration of the worker recovering from long COVID.
4. The primary goal is an appropriate, progressive, and adaptive return to work of a patient recovering from long COVID. An individual is not required to acquire 100% health while returning to work; hence, this approach is useful. To maximize the retention of job of the long COVID patient, the occupational health professionals, both at the clinic/ hospital and the office, shall be actively involved in the entire process.
5. Working has a positive influence on health. One shall be prepared while returning to work to make this return an important step in the rehabilitation process.
6. The occupational health professionals shall collaborate with the employers and healthcare practitioners, developing a trustworthy and fruitful relationship. These professionals play a pivotal role in the return to work of the patients suffering from long COVID.
7. Before returning to the work, the individual shall be briefed about the mental and physical requirements of the job, as

well as a brief of the tasks that the individual will be responsible for. The job characteristics can be altered according to the demands and health condition of the patient.

8. The features of the plan of returning to work include flexible work, strategies for the management of fatigue, time off to accommodate medical appointments and rehabilitation activities, phased return, and adapting work tasks.

Chapter 9 Navigating your Return to Academic Institution

Introduction

Similar to the discussion of a return to work in patients with long COVID, it is also important to elaborate on the return to an academic institution for the students who are suffering from long COVID. As much as professional life is affected by long COVID, the academic life of an individual is also largely influenced by the occurrence of long COVID. This chapter discusses the impact of long COVID on education, the current challenges, and the role of academic institutions in supporting the students recovering from long COVID.

Long COVID and Education

Students suffering from long COVID experience symptoms including lightheadedness, fatigue, and cognitive dysfunction. The coronavirus may influence the neural structures in the affected individuals. This has varying impacts on the motivation, attention, and memory of the patient. Individuals infected with the coronavirus and those who suffer from long COVID also experience other problems, including cardiovascular complications. Chronic stress aggravates the symptoms of long COVID and further deteriorates the overall health of the affected individual. In particular, students who are at a greater risk for chronic stress may also experience the exacerbation of symptoms of long COVID. Owing to the establishment of the COVID-19 pandemic, the students may have also developed traumatic stress, which in turn may exacerbate the symptoms and the overall health condition.

Current Challenges

Stress and the cognitive symptoms of long COVID impose a huge challenge to the academic progress and success of the college students suffering from long COVID. College students may not perform well in their studies and associated exams owing to cognitive issues and persistent deterioration of their health condition. A major obstacle to learning is the chronic fatigue associated with long COVID. The affected students may find it hard to actively focus and engage in learning and academic activities. The development of stress even before the development of COVID-19 infection may contribute to the negative outcomes associated with long COVID. In case of lack of adjustments offered by the academic institutions add to the stress and worsening health condition among the students, which have a significant impact on academic performance of the students. A study revealed that university students, in the light of the COVID-19 pandemic, are concerned about the employment opportunities following graduation.

The Role of Academic Institutions

This section describes the measures that can be undertaken by the academic institutions to promote the return to studies in students suffering from long COVID, as well as provide alternative strategies to promote optimal learning among the students during the pandemic. An important goal of the academic institutions while setting up measures for promoting education in students with long COVID is to minimize mental health problems and enhance academic outcomes.

1. Online Learning Tools

The academic institutions shall establish online learning and provide training to the academic staff accordingly to cater to the students who can't receive education on campus, including the ones who are suffering from long COVID. Not only do the students benefit from online education services, but the teachers suffering from active disease or long COVID may also derive benefits from online learning. The academic institutions may find it challenging to move all or majority of the academic programs online. To overcome this challenge and cope with the pandemic of coronavirus outbreak, the universities shall develop robust systems, thanks to their information technology departments. In addition to the establishment of the online programs, the universities shall also ensure that the online academic program is supported, runs, smoothly, and is adaptable to the varying needs and requirements of the students, particularly the ones who are recovering from long COVID.

1. Assessment of the Issue in the Given Institution

In addition to the introduction, establishment, and maintenance of robust online programs, academic institutions must play an active role in determining the percentage of students who have contracted the infection and those who are suffering from long COVID. The academic institutions may employ confidential surveys to gather relevant data. As per the spread of coronavirus among the students and the number of students suffering from long COVID, the institutions may alter their academic programs and provide resources useful for the recovery and optimal functioning of the affected students. The institutions are also required to engage in conversation with the students to directly inquire about their needs, the current challenges that they face, and their concerns and queries regarding learning.

1. Provide Health and Wellness Services

A more holistic approach is required to effectively manage the onset of long COVID among the students and boost learning among them. This holistic approach is beneficial to the mental health and cognitive functioning of the students, particularly those who are suffering from long COVID. While being on campus, the students shall be encouraged to participate in suitable and appropriate physical activities, which have a positive influence on recovery and mental health. The students shall be offered healthy and nutritious meal options at the campus to promote recovery and improve academic performance.

1. Awareness and Education among the Students

The academic institutions are responsible for educating the students about different aspects of long COVID. The institutions shall demonstrate equity while providing educational opportunities to the students. The institutions shall also identify the disparities and address them appropriately.

1. Collaboration with Healthcare Institutions

The academic institutions may form a partnership with healthcare institutions such as long COVID clinics to provide the necessary resources and therapeutic options. This may cause the resources to become more accessible to the students, which in turn helps the students recover from long COVID, improve their mental health, and boost their academic performance.

Chapter 10 Long COVID in Children – Guide for Parents

Introduction

In addition to adults, children also fall victim to the development of long COVID and the persistence of the associated symptoms. Similar to adults, these symptoms may influence the functioning of the child and affect the quality of life. Children with long COVID are unable to actively engage in routine activities, unlike children who are healthy and carry out routine activities normally. Children with long COVID may also demonstrate symptoms that are pertinent to poor academic function. This chapter will provide parents with useful information about the risk factors, symptoms, similar health conditions, diagnosis, and treatment of long COVID in children.

Prevalence of Long COVID in Children

The prevalence of long COVID among children and adolescents is 25.24%. The prevalent clinical manifestations associated with the development of long COVID include headache, respiratory symptoms, mood symptoms, sleep disorders, and fatigue. In this population, it is difficult to distinguish between pandemic-associated symptoms and the symptoms associated with long COVID. The children who contracted the viral infection are more likely to develop the symptoms of long COVID as compared to children who do not develop the initial coronavirus infection.

Symptoms and Risk Factors of Long COVID in Children

The following symptoms are associated with the development of long COVID in children.

1. Mood swings
2. Stomachaches
3. Rashes
4. Issues with concentration and memory
5. Fatigue
6. Headache
7. Weakness
8. Pain
9. Vision problems
10. Cough
11. Loss of appetite

The symptoms of long COVID in children vary with age of children. In children of ages 0-3, the prevalent symptoms are mood swings, loss of appetite, rashes, stomachaches, and cough. In children of ages 4-11, the prevalent symptoms of long COVID include rashes, difficulties with recall and concentration, and mood swings. Lastly, in children of ages 12-14 years, the prevalent symptoms of long COVID include fatigue, mood swings, and difficulties with recall and concentration.

There are several risk factors associated with the onset of long COVID in the pediatric population. The risk factors may include nutritional status, genetics, prior history of coinfections or recent infections, and the area of inoculation. However, there is a lack of comprehensive knowledge about the risk factors of long COVID among children. Hence, further research is required to fill the knowledge gap.

The symptoms of long COVID may also overlap with the symptoms of other health conditions in children. For instance, the symptoms of chronic fatigue syndrome may mimic the symptoms of long COVID. These symptoms include brain fog, intense lightheadedness, post-exertional malaise (PEM), and fatigue. PEM is associated with the excessive mental or physical activity performed by the child. Children with long COVID may suffer from orthostatic intolerance, which may cause weakness, dizziness, and lightheadedness. Orthostatic intolerance is a manifestation of reduced flow of blood to the brain of the child. This causes the child to have low levels of energy and elicits the need to rest after certain physical activities.

The symptoms of long COVID in children are usually mild and are associated with a paradoxical greater quality of life. The recent strains of coronavirus seem to cause symptoms of long COVID that are less severe in children. Previous infections with the coronavirus cause the children to develop immunity against the coronavirus. Moreover, the symptoms in children with long COVID are likely to be associated with health conditions apart from COVID-19. Even if the symptoms appearing in children with long COVID, are related to COVID-19, the symptoms eventually pass with time.

Diagnosis and Treatment of Long COVID in Children

Similar to the diagnosis of long COVID in other populations, there are no definite tests available for the diagnosis of long COVID in children. The healthcare provider constructs the diagnosis based on the symptoms evident in the children suffering from long COVID. The symptoms of long COVID persist for a longer duration and hinder the routine functioning of the child. The healthcare provider shall obtain information about the type and duration of the symptoms, previous onset of coronavirus infection, and other underlying health conditions in the affected child. The healthcare provider may also inquire about the academic performance of the child to assess the cognitive function of the child.

The presence of COVID-19 antibodies in the child is indicative of prior infection or appears following the administration of the COVID-19 vaccine.

The most common concern in parents with children suffering from long COVID is about the treatment of this health condition. The confirmation of the diagnosis is important to the treatment plan for long COVID in children. The doctor may run other tests and evaluations to rule out other probable causes of the symptoms that the child presents with. The children must be encouraged to rest and consume a healthy and well-balanced diet. Specific pharmacological interventions are not often offered to the children, as the symptoms are mild and resolve on their own. To further promote recovery and acquisition of optimal health, there is a dire need for an established network comprising home, school, daycare, and a clinical facility if any. The children must be offered comprehensive and integrative care for proper management of the symptoms. Children with other underlying health conditions shall be offered treatment for that particular health condition as well so that they can attain optimal health.

Parents play a pivotal role in the prevention, treatment, and management of long COVID in children. The parents must ensure the establishment and implementation of protective measures such as social distancing and hygiene to prevent the onset of COVID-19 infection and subsequent development of long COVID in the children. The schools and daycare centers shall offer adequate support to the parents and children by accommodating their requirements and addressing the issues that the parents and children are facing. The parents shall also assist their children in getting the vaccine so that they develop sufficient immunity against the virus. The duration of persistence of symptoms vary from child to child, however, these symptoms undergo complete or partial resolution over the passage of time. Psychological interventions in addition to adequate rest are also useful for helping the children to cope with the symptoms of long COVID. Further research studies are required to investigate the symptoms, risk factors, diagnosis, and therapeutic measures in children suffering from long COVID.

References

Chandan, J. S., Brown, K., Simms-Williams, N., Camaradou, J., Bashir, N., Heining, D., Aiyegbusi, O. L., Turner, G., Cruz Rivera, S., Hotham, R., Nirantharakumar, K., Sivan, M., Khunti, K., Raindi, D., Marwaha, S., Hughes, S. E., McMullan, C., Calvert, M., & Haroon, S. (2022). Non-pharmacological therapies for postviral syndromes, including Long COVID: a systematic review and meta-analysis protocol. *BMJ Open*, *12*(4), e057885. https://doi.org/10.1136/bmjopen-2021-057885

The Lancet. (2021). Understanding long COVID: a modern medical challenge. *The Lancet*, *398*(10302), 725. https://doi.org/10.1016/s0140-6736(21)01900-0

van Kessel, S. A. M., Olde Hartman, T. C., Lucassen, P. L. B. J., & van Jaarsveld, C. H. M. (2021). Post-acute and long-COVID-19 symptoms in patients with mild diseases: a systematic review. *Family Practice*, *39*(1), 159–167. https://doi.org/10.1093/fampra/cmab076

Al-Aly, Z., Bowe, B., & Xie, Y. (2022). Long COVID after breakthrough SARS-CoV-2 infection. *Nature Medicine*, *28*(7), 1461–1467. https://doi.org/10.1038/s41591-022-01840-0

Daines, L., Zheng, B., Pfeffer, P., Hurst, J. R., & Sheikh, A. (2022). A clinical review of long-COVID with a focus on the respiratory system. *Current Opinion in Pulmonary Medicine, 28*(3), 174–179. https://doi.org/10.1097/mcp.0000000000000863

Rajan. (2021). *In the wake of the pandemic: Preparing for Long COVID [Internet].* https://pubmed.ncbi.nlm.nih.gov/33877759/

Rajan. (2021). *In the wake of the pandemic: Preparing for Long COVID [Internet].* https://pubmed.ncbi.nlm.nih.gov/33877759/

Raveendran, A. V., Jayadevan, R., & Sashidharan, S. (2021). Long COVID: An overview. *Diabetes & Metabolic Syndrome: Clinical Research & Reviews, 15*(3), 869–875. https://doi.org/10.1016/j.dsx.2021.04.007

Jarrott, B., Head, R., Pringle, K. G., Lumbers, E. R., & Martin, J. H. (2022). "LONG COVID"—A hypothesis for understanding the biological basis and pharmacological treatment strategy. *Pharmacology Research & Perspectives, 10*(1). https://doi.org/10.1002/prp2.911

Meagher, T. (2022). Long COVID – One Year On. *Journal of Insurance Medicine.* https://doi.org/10.17849/insm-49-3-1-6.1

Lopez-Leon, S., Wegman-Ostrosky, T., Perelman, C., Sepulveda, R., Rebolledo, P. A., Cuapio, A., & Villapol, S. (2021). *More than 50 Long-term effects of COVID-19: a systematic review and meta-analysis.* https://doi.org/10.1101/2021.01.27.21250617

Chen, C., Haupert, S. R., Zimmermann, L., Shi, X., Fritsche, L. G., & Mukherjee, B. (2022). Global Prevalence of Post-Coronavirus Disease 2019 (COVID-19) Condition or Long COVID: A Meta-Analysis and Systematic Review. *The Journal of Infectious Diseases.* https://doi.org/10.1093/infdis/jiac136

Castanares-Zapatero, D., Chalon, P., Kohn, L., Dauvrin, M., Detollenaere, J., Maertens de Noordhout, C., Primus-de Jong, C., Cleemput, I., & Van den Heede, K. (2022). Pathophysiology and mechanism of long COVID: a comprehensive review. *Annals of Medicine, 54*(1), 1473–1487. https://doi.org/10.1080/07853890.2022.2076901

Ziauddeen, N., Gurdasani, D., O'Hara, M. E., Hastie, C., Roderick, P., Yao, G., & Alwan, N. A. (2022). Characteristics and impact of Long Covid: Findings from an online survey. *PLOS ONE*, *17*(3), e0264331. https://doi.org/10.1371/journal.pone.0264331

Aiyegbusi, O. L., Hughes, S. E., Turner, G., Rivera, S. C., McMullan, C., Chandan, J. S., Haroon, S., Price, G., Davies, E. H., Nirantharakumar, K., Sapey, E., & Calvert, M. J. (2021). Symptoms, complications and management of long COVID: a review. *Journal of the Royal Society of Medicine*, *114*(9), 428–442. https://doi.org/10.1177/01410768211032850

Yan, Z., Yang, M., & Lai, C.-L. (2021). Long COVID-19 Syndrome: A Comprehensive Review of Its Effect on Various Organ Systems and Recommendation on Rehabilitation Plans. *Biomedicines*, *9*(8), 966. https://doi.org/10.3390/biomedicines9080966

Crook, H., Raza, S., Nowell, J., Young, M., & Edison, P. (2021). Long covid—mechanisms, risk factors, and management. *BMJ*, n1648. https://doi.org/10.1136/bmj.n1648

Raveendran, A. V., Jayadevan, R., & Sashidharan, S. (2021). Long COVID: An overview. *Diabetes & Metabolic Syndrome: Clinical Research & Reviews, 15*(3), 869–875. https://doi.org/10.1016/j.dsx.2021.04.007

About the Author

Jean-Maurice Cecilia-Menzel is an alternative practitioner of psychotherapy and a trained neurofeedback therapist. A three-year degree in health and social care, two years of training in psychotherapeutic work and ongoing research round off his career to date. He practices as an alternative practitioner of psychotherapy in his own office in Munich.

Read more at https://www.neurofeedback-praxis-muenchen.de.